Corgis
at Work

Sabrina Lakes

Herding Dogs

**PAWS &
PASTURES**

at Work

x*ist Publishing

Check out all of the books in the Paws and Pastures Series

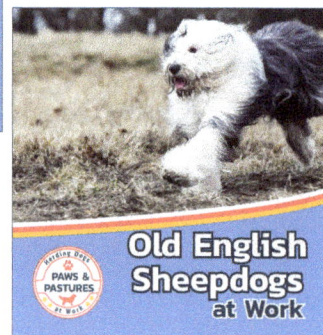

Australian Shepherds at Work

Collies at Work

Corggies at Work

Old English Sheepdogs at Work

Published in the United States by Xist Publishing
www.xistpublishing.com
© 2025 Copyright Xist Publishing

First Edition
Hardcover ISBN: 978-1-5324-5547-6
Paperback ISBN: 978-1-5324-5548-3
eISBN: 978-1-5324-5546-9

PUBLISHED IN TEXAS

Table of Contents

Introduction to Corgis

Corgis are small dogs. They have short legs and long bodies. They come from Wales. Farmers used them to help with animals. Corgis are smart and friendly. They love to play and work hard.

Fun Facts About Corgis

Corgis have a lot of energy. They can run fast, even with short legs. Corgis have big ears that stand up straight. Their fluffy tails wag when they are happy. Many people love Corgis because they are so cute.

What is Herding?

Herding means guiding animals like sheep or cows. Corgis help farmers keep animals in groups. They move the animals to new places. This job is very important on farms.

Why Corgis are Great Herders?

Corgis are great herders because they are smart. They learn quickly and follow orders. Their short legs help them move fast and low to the ground. This helps them nip at the animals' heels to keep them moving. Corgis are also very brave and strong.

Training a Corgi

Training a Corgi is fun and easy. Start with simple commands like "sit" and "stay." Use treats to reward good behavior. Be patient and kind. Corgis love to learn new things.

Games to Help Corgis Learn

Games make training fun for Corgis. Play fetch to teach them to come back. Hide treats and let them find them. This helps them use their noses and brains. Another game is herding a ball, which is like herding animals.

13

A Day in the Life of a Herding Corgi

Corgis start their day early. They eat breakfast and get ready. Then, they help the farmer with the animals. They guide the sheep or cows to the fields. Corgis are always busy.

Working with the Animals

Corgis work hard all day. They keep the animals together and safe. They run around and make sure no animals get lost. Corgis use their barks and nips to move the animals. They are very good at their job.

Caring for a Corgi

Corgis need good food to stay strong. They eat healthy meals twice a day. Brushing their fur keeps it shiny and clean. Corgis also need their nails trimmed regularly. This helps them walk and run better.

Keeping Your Corgi Healthy

Corgis need exercise every day. Walks and playtime are important. They also need check-ups at the vet. This keeps them happy and healthy. Corgis love to be active and busy.

21

Corgis at Rest

After working hard, Corgis need rest. They like to nap in cozy spots. Resting helps them recharge for the next day. Corgis also enjoy cuddling with their owners.

23

Fun Activities for Corgis

Corgis love to play, even when they are resting. They enjoy toys that squeak or bounce. Puzzle toys keep their minds busy. Spending time with their family makes them happiest of all.

Glossary

Check-up   A visit to the vet to make sure a pet is healthy.

Commands   Words or signals used to tell a dog what to do, like "sit" or "stay."

Exercise   Activities like walking or playing that help keep a dog strong and fit.

Grooming   Taking care of a dog's fur and nails to keep them clean and healthy.

Herding   Guiding and moving animals like sheep or cows.

Nutritious   Food that is healthy and good for growth and strength.

Puzzle Toys   Toys that challenge a dog's mind and keep them entertained.

Recharge   Resting to get energy back after working or playing.

Treats   Special food given to dogs as a reward for good behavior.

Index

Index

Keyword List

Nouns	Verbs	Adjectives	Adverbs
animal	are	brave	better
body	come	busy	easily
command	follow	clean	every
cow	guide	cute	day
corgi	have	early	fast
dog	help	fluffy	low
ear	keep	friendly	quickly
energy	learn	good	regularly
fact	love	great	safely
farmer	meet	happy	
farm	move	hard	
fun	nip	healthy	
ground	play	long	
heel	reward	new	
job	run	shiny	
leg	stand	short	
people	train	simple	
sheep	used	small	
tail	wag	smart	
Wales	work	strong	

Herding Dogs

PAWS &
PASTURES

at Work

www.ingramcontent.com/pod-product-compliance
Lightning Source LLC
LaVergne TN
LVHW070835080426
835508LV00031B/3470

9 781532 455483